WEAPONIZED

SOCIAL

MEDIA

Sherri M. Gordon

Enslow Publishing
101 W. 23rd Street
Suite 240
New York, NY 10011
USA

enslow.com

Published in 2019 by Enslow Publishing, LLC.
101 W. 23rd Street, Suite 240, New York, NY 1001

Library of Congress Cataloging-in-Publication Data

Names: Gordon, Sherri M., author.
Title: Weaponized social media / Sherri M. Gordon.
Description: New York : Enslow Publishing, [2019] | Series: Critical thinking about digital media | Audience: Grades 7–12. | Includes bibliographical references and index.
Identifiers: LCCN 2018020368| ISBN 9781978504752 (library bound) | ISBN 9781978505704 (pbk.)
Subjects: LCSH: Social media—Social aspects. | Cyberbullying.
Classification: LCC HM742 .G68 2018 | DDC 302.23/1—dc23
LC record available at https://lccn.loc.gov/2018020368

Printed in the United States of America

To Our Readers: We have done our best to make sure all website addresses in this book were active and appropriate when we went to press. However, the author and the publisher have no control over and assume no liability for the material available on those websites or on any websites they may link to. Any comments or suggestions can be sent by email to customerservice@enslow.com.

CONTENTS

INTRODUCTION

Courtney Allen's troubles began after she tried to end a relationship with Todd, a man she met through an online gaming site. After a year of building an online relationship with Todd, Courtney's husband, Steven, found out about their affair. Eventually, Courtney severed her relationship with Todd, but Todd was furious and wanted revenge.

In the beginning, Courtney says her relationship with Todd was an escape. "He was charming. He told me everything that I ever wanted to hear about how wonderful I was," she says. "...Because it was online, it was very easy to not see the faults someone has, to not see the warning signs."

For Courtney, her experience with social media left her feeling trapped in a world of anonymous abuse. Not only was she paralyzed with fear of what would be posted next, but she also had no idea how to make it stop. Even involving the police did very little to bring an end to the harassment. Plus, she was concerned that the people in her life believed the posts and accusations about her.

To complicate matters, Courtney and Todd shared explicit photos and videos during their relationship. These images were what Todd used as weapons to shame and harass

Courtney and Steven through social media. Todd started a fake Facebook account under Steven's name with a nude photograph of Courtney as the profile picture. This caused her inbox to fill with nasty messages, some of which even included death threats.

Courtney's coworkers received emails with videos and screenshots of Courtney naked. The messages came from different email addresses, some made to look like Steven had sent them. From there, the harassment became even more personal. Local child protective services received an anonymous call that Steven was abusing their son, which resulted in an investigation. Courtney and Steven also received an anonymous package of marijuana in the mail. After contacting police, a local detective told them that they had been accused of selling the drug to high school students. Their credit cards were even used fraudulently, and they received harassing phone calls daily.

Courtney and Steven tried involving the police, including filing a protection order against Todd. There was not much law enforcement could do, so the couple contacted a law firm designed to help victims of harassment, settling with their harassers, and getting the images off the internet.

The attorneys found countless social media accounts impersonating them, and even one account impersonating their 4-year-old son. Every time sites would be taken down new ones would pop up. The impersonators often used sophisticated anonymizers to make the accounts harder to trace. By the time the case went to trial, the attorneys had compiled 1,083 exhibits, including an 83-page chart to organize the emails

Todd had sent. Eventually, a jury found Todd guilty of everything from harassment to impersonation.[1]

Many people assume that being harassed online is something easy to avoid. But weaponized social media is more common than you might think. One study found that one in every twenty-five Americans online, or about ten million people, had either explicit photos of them shared online against their will or at least was threatened to have them shared. For women younger than thirty, the rate at which explicit photos are shared jumps to one in ten. These numbers do not include the countless governments, politicians, political groups, and more that weaponize social media every day.[2]

"Nobody is safe," Courtney Allen says. "If you're on [social media], you're pretty much a target."[3]

Then and Now: A Closer Look at Social Media

People are social creatures. As a result, they crave social experiences—communities where they can create connections and build memories. Social media may have started with BBSs (bulletin board systems), but in the 1990s, when better platforms arrived, promising more connection and community, people were quick to adapt.

The first true social media site was Six Degrees, which existed from 1997 to 2001. It was named after the "six degrees of separation theory," which states that anyone on the planet can be connected to anyone else in as few as six steps. Much like the social media sites of today, Six Degrees allowed users to create a profile and friend other people. It even allowed people who did not register with the site to confirm friendships or connections.

Social media expanded to include blogging and instant messaging before morphing into the social media sites we have today. By the early 2000s, sites like MySpace, a smaller version of Facebook and popular among musicians, started

It doesn't matter what platform you're on. From Facebook to Instagram, social media can be turned against you.

gaining popularity, while LinkedIn gained traction among working professionals who wanted to connect online.

Facebook began as TheFacebook in 2004, available only to Harvard University students, but after seeing its potential, creator Mark Zuckerberg released the service to the world. Around the same time, the popularity of text messaging inspired Jack Dorsey and several others to create Twitter for

2003: MySpace
2004: TheFacebook and Flickr
2005: YouTube
2006: Twitter, PopSugar, Facebook goes public
2007: Tumblr
2010: Pinterest, Instagram, iTunes Ping
2011: Google+, SnapChat, Nextdoor
2013: Vine
2014: Ello

short "tweets" of 140 characters or less. Today, these two sites are among the most popular social networks on the internet. Facebook is the number one social media site, boasting over a billion users, while Twitter has more than 500 million users.

Instagram, Photobucket, and Flickr helped jump-start photo sharing, and YouTube arrived in 2005 allowing people to share videos. Other sites like Pinterest, Tumblr, and Foursquare filled other specific niches for users.

Social media also started to become a widespread tool for businesses, organizations, and other groups. Today, it is not uncommon for businesses to list their social media addresses on their advertising materials and websites. Businesses and organizations without social media sites are considered old fashioned or behind the times.[1]

Why People "Like" Social Media

The internet has changed the way people, especially young adults, view the world. To many, the online world is the real world. Not only has interacting on social media sites reduced the size of the world around us, but it also has put the world

Staying in touch with friends through social media is no longer revolutionary. It's a part of everyday life: 78 percent of teens say it makes them feel closer to friends.

at our fingertips. We can communicate with friends near and far, share our lives, read the news, and follow our favorite musicians all from the comfort of our home.

People have embraced social media as the new normal, especially teens. A study by the Associated Press and NORC at the University of Chicago found that 78 percent of young adults ages thirteen to seventeen who use social media say it makes them feel closer to friends. Forty percent say social media makes them feel closer to family. Almost half of teens indicate that social media makes them feel more informed.[2]

No longer do teens have to rely on snail mail, landlines, and other outdated forms of communication to connect with their friends. Instead, they have a way to communicate anytime they want, day or night, by pulling out their smartphone.

How Social Media Has Changed Us

With more than 78 percent of Americans maintaining a social media profile of some sort, social media not only impacts how we spend our time, but also how we feel about ourselves. As people's lives become increasingly more public, they tend to think in terms of their "personal brand" when posting and interacting online.

"I love using social media to share more of my personal life with my network," says Deena Baikowitz, chief networking officer at Fireball Network. "It makes me—and everyone who uses it—more memorable, relatable, interesting and approachable."

Baikowitz says that at business events people will make comments about her posts, asking her about her dating life or commenting on how much they love her photos. "Sharing my personal life creates much more meaningful connections, provides fun conversation starters, and sets a friendly tone to lead into business talk."

But there are other concerns with sharing your life online. "I find myself being thoughtful in what I respond to, share or state as it not only reflects on [me personally] but the brand I represent and I would not want one of my posts misinterpreted," explains Dea Lawrence, the CMO of *Variety*.[3]

Everything you say online can be easily misinterpreted because text often won't carry your tone the way spoken words will. Consider what you post.

There is a downside to sharing your personal life online, too. Sometimes people do not always interpret the things you post or share in the way you intended. Jokes and sarcasm in particular are hard to recognize online. People cannot see your face or hear your tone of voice, so it is easy for things to be misinterpreted. Some find it difficult to be authentic online and instead are always focused on what kind of message they are sending about themselves or how they might be impacting their "personal brand."

Social Media Today: The Good and the Bad

There is no doubt that social media has become a powerful tool to organize and mobilize massive groups of likeminded people. Much good has come from connecting people around the world; it allows people to share their message with a broader audience and get help when needed.[4]

But many people do not realize the "leakiness" of these information databases, says Danielle Citron, a law professor at the University of Maryland and author of *Hate Crimes in Cyberspace*. She says nearly everyone is sharing private information without understanding how it might be used. From workout apps that generate maps to our homes and harmless-seeming quizzes that reveal personal information, to geotagged photos and Facebook updates revealing when and where we are, we are leaving an enormous digital trail of personal information.

"People are just starting to understand that the web watches them back," says Aleecia McDonald, a privacy researcher at Stanford's Center for Internet and Society. Still,

As the saying goes: the internet is forever. Think of the internet as a time machine that you load with ammunition every time you post something.

she says people do not understand the risks they might face in the future by sharing information through social media. She suggests thinking of the internet as a time machine that we are constantly loading with ammunition.

"Everything that's on file about you for the last 15 years and the next 40 years may someday be used against you," she warns.[5]

GETTING OFF TRACK: THE IMPACT OF WEAPONIZED SOCIAL MEDIA

The goal of social media pioneers like Mark Zuckerberg (Facebook) and Jack Dorsey (Twitter) was to connect people around the world. They felt by allowing people to connect and share information, they would help make the world a better place. While in many respects that has happened, there also is a much darker side to social media.

Comprised of armies of bots, trolls, and story spinners, there are groups of people who exploit social media and use it to change public opinion, whitewash stories, and poison debates. They sell a story to the masses that is often untrue in order to accomplish their goals.

One place where this is evident is in Myanmar, a small sovereign state in Southeast Asia. There, social media has been weaponized against the Rohingya minority, an ethnic group comprised mostly of Muslims. In Myanmar, the ruling regime,

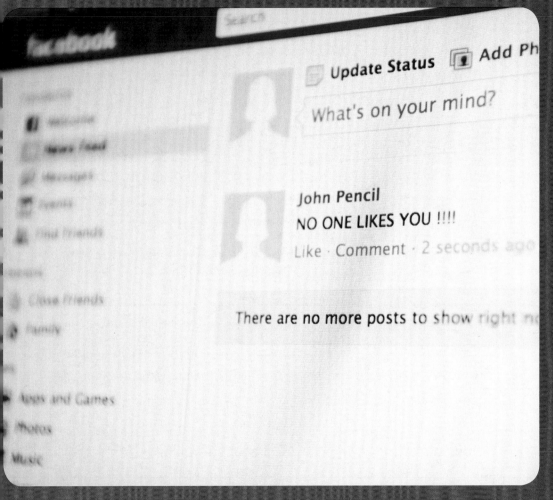

As fun as the internet can be, there is a darker side of the online community, containing trolls, fake news, and harassment.

comprised mostly of Buddhists, is carrying out what some UN officials call a "textbook example of ethnic cleansing."

The regime has launched a deadly attack, slaughtering men, women, and children, and burning hundreds of villages to the ground. Nearly 700,000 Rohingya have fled their homes to take refuge in camps across the border in Bangladesh.

Social media has been "one of the most damaging aspects of this entire crisis," says David Mathieson, an independent analyst who has lived and worked in the region for years. Buddhist nationalists use Facebook to spread lies about the Rohingya. Not only do they minimize and deny allegations about human rights abuses, but they also suggest that the Rohingya have burned their villages.

"The government's main plan is ... to carry out slow and steady genocide and to wipe out this minority, clearly," says a thirty-year-old Rohingya refugee who is part of a group of journalists who work to smuggle news and video of atrocities to the outside world.[1]

Clint Watts, a senior fellow at the Center for Cyber and Homeland Security at George Washington University, says the more times you see a message, the more likely you are to believe it. As a result, social media weaponization can create false worlds in the social media space.[2]

Reading People's Minds

One of the reasons social media is such a useful tool for spreading misinformation and influencing public opinion is that the people bent on weaponizing it are able to leverage

Everything you do online has a value to someone. When you fill out a form, like a post, or take a personality quiz, this information is collected and kept.

the large amounts of data that social media platforms like Facebook collect.

One way they do this is by using psychological targeting techniques. They can develop psychological profiles based on what people like or who they follow on social media. With a psychological profile in hand, data analysts can use the information collected to "nudge" individuals into doing or believing what they want them to.

Cambridge Analytica is one company that allegedly did just that. Prior to the 2016 US presidential election, the company gathered private information from the Facebook profiles of more than fifty million users without their permission. Aside from being one of the largest data leaks in the history of Facebook, the breach allowed the company to use private social media activity for potential political gains.

With the help of a psychology professor, Dr. Kogan, Cambridge Analytica built an app that helped them map personality traits based on what people liked on Facebook. Most people who took their quizzes thought the data was being used for academic research. In reality, it was being used to build psychographic profiles.

The information Dr. Kogan gathered provided the company with personal information, including where people lived. With this data in hand, they could not only identify where people lived and if they were registered to vote, but also zero in on their hot-button issues and exploit them. Although it is unclear how the psychographic data was used during President Donald Trump's campaign, experts speculate that it could have been used to help sway voters.[3]

The Problem with Being Like-Minded

Your newsfeed on Facebook, Twitter, and other social media sites uses algorithms designed to show you information that you should like. If the application can identify the content you like and show you more of it, you will be happier with your experience.

Not necessarily, says Harvard Law School professor Cass R. Sunstein. Those algorithms create an "information cocoon." When people are exposed only to those beliefs that reflect their own, those beliefs tend to push them toward extreme viewpoints.

Sunstein says that engaging online with only like-minded people and information can widen the gap between different groups. This is especially true for people who have different political views. [5]

Individuals, governments, and companies that weaponize social media and digital technologies are creating messages and programs that are "designed to exploit our psychological vulnerabilities in order to direct us toward goals that may or may not align with our own," explains James Williams, a former Google advertising executive.[4]

How Social Media Hijacks the Brain

Most people think they can spot fake news and misinformation. They want to believe they are in control of their thought processes. The problem with social media is that it makes it too easy for our thought processes to bypass the rational part of our brains. Social media encourages emotional, reactive, and "quick-fix" responses. What's more, it appeals to our brain's preference for interesting images as well as clicks or likes that feed our egos.

These emotional responses come at the expense of deep thinking, planning, and interaction. This doesn't mean that people cannot have thought-provoking debates online. They can and do. But there is a tendency to move away from rational debates and instead focus on strong emotional responses.

One explanation for this phenomenon is offered by Daniel Kahneman, Nobel Prize-winning behavioral economist, and Richard Thaler, a Pulitzer Prize winner. Together, they have given classes to executives at Google, Twitter, and Facebook in "Thinking, About Thinking."

Their goal is to bring awareness to the fact that there are two types of thinking, System 1 and System 2. System 1 thinking is "fast" thinking: automatic, emotional, and subconscious.

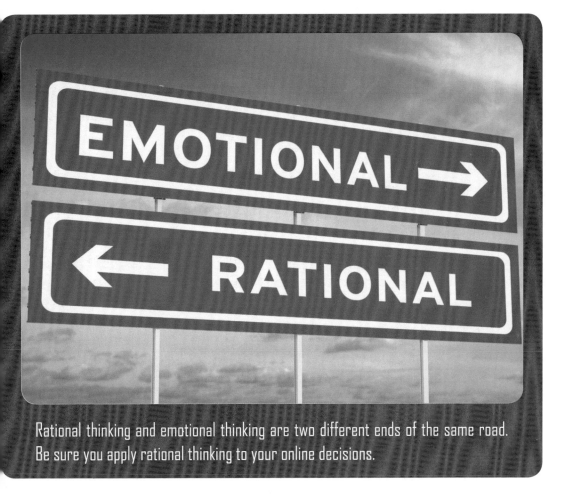

Rational thinking and emotional thinking are two different ends of the same road. Be sure you apply rational thinking to your online decisions.

System 2 thinking involves "slow" thinking, which requires effort. It is logical, calculating, and conscious.

Facebook, Twitter, and other social media outlets are built on System 1 thinking. Social media primes us to use System 1 thinking for issues we know require System 2 thinking, such as considering political candidates or making informed decisions about important issues like gun control. Some experts argue that the world is becoming less democratic in the wake of social media. Even Sean Parker, former president of Facebook, admits that Facebook and other social media sites are not as altruistic as society had hoped.

"Social media is a social validation feedback loop," Parker says, "...exactly the kind of thing a hacker like myself would come up with, because you're exploiting a vulnerability in human psychology."[6]

Online Danger Zone: How Social Media Is Weaponized by Teens

When Francie was thirteen, she had falling out with her best friend, Amanda. After they parted ways, Amanda used technology and the internet to torture Francie for the next three years.

Because the two had been inseparable and shared everything, Amanda was able to hack into Francie's accounts with ease, even after Francie changed her password. Their one-time bond as best friends had provided Amanda with all the information she needed to figure out passwords or answer security questions.

"The worst part was the calendar reminders," Francie shares with the *Atlantic*. "Written in the first person, they notified me of my own plans to kill myself. I would be quietly browsing, then the reminder would pop up: 'Throw myself off the …bridge.' These reminders were always set for midnight, in the dead of winter. I was an imaginative child, so they would

Social media has changed the way friends interact and the way they argue. Everything you post online can be used against you, especially by friends who know you best.

bring up the whole scene for me immediately: I would see my own hands on the bridge railing, the darkness of the water below."[1]

Even though Francie felt alone and anxious, she was able to get through the harassment and abuse. Unfortunately, some young adults who have social media weaponized against them do not survive the torture.

Ways Teens Are Weaponizing Social Media

When it comes to bullying, harassing, and controlling other people, many teenagers have turned to social media. Not only

Signs Social Media Is Hurting Your Friendship

- **Feeling left out.** A healthy friendship involves people who are inclusive, but people are not necessarily being mean every time you are not invited. Sometimes there are other reasons why you weren't included, such as being required to limit the number of invites by parents.
- **Disagreements are played out online.** Friends who fight online, tweet about you, or post about your disagreement on social media are not being good friends. Disagreements should always be handled offline and in person.
- **Your friend posts inappropriate content or makes rude comments.** If you have a friend who posts hateful comments, rude posts, or spreads rumors, this is not a reflection of a good friend.[2]

have they discovered that they can do it from the privacy of their own home, but they have found that hiding behind a computer screen can give them a false sense of courage. They feel like they are anonymous—that no one knows who they are.

Two of the most popular ways in which kids are weaponizing social media is through cyberbullying and trolling. Although it is easy to confuse cyberbullying and trolling, their goals are actually quite different. Trolls are looking to create a disruption online and will target anyone in their path in order to accomplish

Cyberbullies tend to target specific people with their hate, whereas trolls take a broader brush with their harassment to create any kind of upset.

this goal. Cyberbullies target specific people with their mean words and hateful posts. They set out to shame, humiliate, and intimidate people. Here is a closer look at both.

How Cyberbullies Are Weaponizing Social Media

Today's cyberbullies often use a variety of methods. These methods can include something as basic as harassing someone online to something more complex such as impersonating the intended target. Here is an overview of the most common methods cyberbullies use to turn social media into a weapon they use against their peers.

Harass the Target on Social Media

When it comes to using social media to harass someone, there are a variety of tactics that cyberbullies use. These include:

- Using direct messages or posts to harass, threaten, or embarrass the target.
- Posting rumors, threats, or embarrassing information on social media.
- Engaging in "warning wars." Most social media sites allow users to report people who are saying inappropriate things. As a result, cyberbullies often push another person until they say something inappropriate and then they report the target to the site. This sometimes results in a person being banned or suspended.
- Shaming the person on social media either with videos or photos.

Impersonate the Target on Social Media

It is not uncommon for kids to pretend to be someone they are not online. But when they go so far as to pretend to be another person in order to create chaos in that person's life, it borders on criminal. Here are some ways kids are impersonating others online:

- Develop a screen name similar to the target's and then make rude, false, and hurtful comments online.
- Steal the target's password or login information and make mean or vile posts. They might message other people while pretending to be the target in attempt to fracture relationships with peers, friends, and family.
- Hack into the target's profile and change it to include sexual photos, racist comments, and hate speech.
- Establish a fake account on social media and pose as the target. The cyberbully will then say mean, rude, and hurtful things and everyone believes the target is making those posts. Real photos of the target are often used to make the account look even more authentic.
- Pretend to be a love interest to lure someone into a fake relationship, then expose the person on social media with the goal of humiliating and embarrassing the person. This is known as "catfishing."

Use Photographs as Weapons on Social Media

Sometimes cyberbullies will use embarrassing or humiliating photographs in order to shame someone on social media. Here are some ways in which photos can become weapons:

On social media, photographs can become weapons when someone posts a degrading or unflattering image. Having a bad hair day? Someone may post a snapshot with a nasty caption.

- Snapping nude or degrading photos of the target without their permission. This might take place in a locker room, bathroom, or dressing room.
- Threatening the target with embarrassing photos as a way of manipulating them into doing what the cyberbully wants.
- Posting and sharing nude or sexually explicit photos on social media for anyone to see and download.
- Use photos as a tool to shame someone online. One example is slut shaming, which involves ridiculing someone for the way they dress or act, or how much they date.

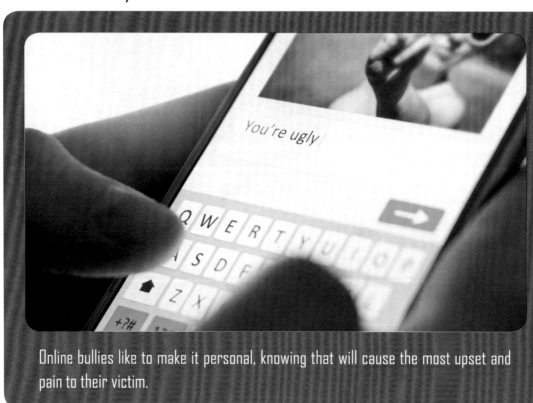

Online bullies like to make it personal, knowing that will cause the most upset and pain to their victim.

Create Polls, Blogs, and Websites

Cyberbullies who are dedicated to shaming, harassing, and humiliating their target will invest time in creating online platforms like polls or blogs and turn them into weapons. This way, they can get other people to participate in the harassment. Here are some examples of what they might do:

- Devote a website or blog to sharing humiliating, personal, or embarrassing information about the target.
- Develop and conduct a poll about the target. Questions might include something like "hot or not" or "fat or thin" and so on.
- Start rumors and tell lies about the target through online websites or blogs.
- Share the target's personal information and photos on a dating website, which puts the target at risk for being contacted by predators.
- Use information that was shared in private to embarrass the target publicly.
- Post mean, hurtful, or insulting comments about the target via the chat option on online gaming sites.
- Sending viruses, spyware, or hacking programs to the target in order to spy on them or control their digital devices remotely.[3]

How Trolls Are Weaponizing Social Media

When it comes to trolling, you will typically find trolls on Twitter, YouTube, and public social media pages looking for opportunities to attack other people.

A troll's primary goal is to attract attention and disrupt online conversations. The more chaos and disruption they can cause, the happier they are. They get a great deal of enjoyment from attacking other people online and upsetting people and hijacking conversations. Here is an overview of the most common methods used by trolls:

- **Trolls make it personal.** Once a troll decides to target you, everything you say or do online becomes ammunition for their attacks. They do this by insulting you, humiliating you, and making you feel bad about yourself.

- **Trolls make painful accusations.** Breaking you down and torturing you is a troll's specialty. They also twist your online statements to mean something other than what was intended and try to discredit every aspect of your viewpoint. No matter what you say, trolls question you as a person. In the end, you are left doubting who you are and what you believe in.

- **Trolls want to destroy you.** As a result, they will never recognize anything good about you. Their approach is one-sided and irrational, and they refuse to look at you objectively. Instead, they want to undermine you in every way they can.

- **Trolls make unfair assumptions about you.** Trolls will look for every opportunity to engage in character assassination. They might call you crazy or a moron. Not only are they twisting your words, but they are attaching an unfair label as well.

- **Trolls tell lies.** Even when you show where they are wrong or lying, they will stick to their story. The more you or others call them out on their lies, the more fun they have. Remember, they do not care about being right. Their goal is to create chaos.
- **Trolls have little regard for online rules.** You might as well throw out the online rules for commenting and posting because trolls refuse to follow them. Often, if they do get kicked off a social media site, they will just come back with a different username.
- **Trolls use crude language.** When trolls use profanity and derogatory language, they are trying to upset you. Trolls recognize these words are powerful and often use them.
- **Trolls fire off their posts and comments at a rapid pace.** Most trolls have large blocks of time during which they start fights online. Because they feed on the drama, they rarely step away from their screens.[4]

Blurred Lines

In cyberspace, it is easy to blur the line between what is acceptable and what is not. After all, you are often alone and behind a screen with no one to hold you accountable until after you've commented or posted. You cannot see the damage you may cause because you do not see the person on the other side of the screen. Nor can you see the faces of the countless others who read what you have said.

For this reason, it becomes increasingly easy to become callous and lacking in empathy. To you, your posts may seem like such a small part of the fast-moving world of social media. What was a big deal the other day is quickly replaced by the next big scandal, and soon online mistakes are forgotten— unless someone is keeping tabs and chooses to use it against you in the future.

Information Warfare: How Social Media Is Being Weaponized by Governments, Politicians, and Businesses

In the wake of fake news, misinformation campaigns, and Russian bots interfering with the 2016 US presidential election, people are starting to realize that social media is much more dangerous than it used to be. One of the most popular Texas secession web pages in the country, "Heart of Texas," had nearly a quarter of a million followers, and views in the billions, before it was discovered to be a Russian-created page. But the people liking, following, and sharing the page's information had no idea.

The goal behind "Heart of Texas" was simple—to use the country's hot issues such as racism, gun control, and immigration

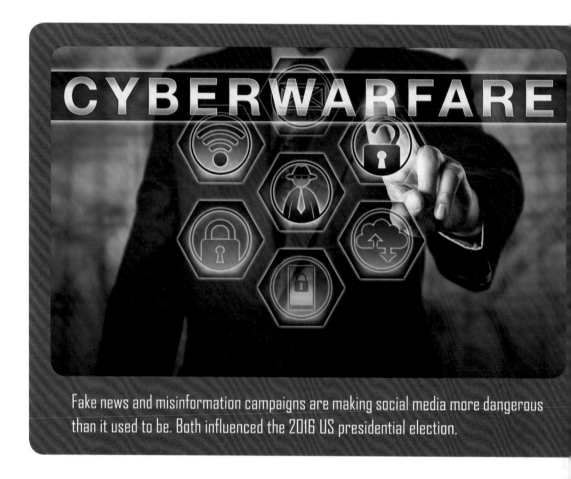

Fake news and misinformation campaigns are making social media more dangerous than it used to be. Both influenced the 2016 US presidential election.

to increase tensions in the United States. When Facebook discovered that the page was a Russian front operated by the notorious Internet Research Agency, they shut it down.

At one point, the site had more followers than the official Texas Democrat and official Texas Republican Facebook pages combined. The Internet Research Agency played Americans for fools. Even though the site's authors clearly understood their audience, their writings and posts were filled with spelling and grammatical errors. These errors didn't create enough suspicion to keep people from following them.[1]

How Weaponizers Are Getting People Hooked

During the 2016 election, Donald Trump discovered that social media does not require facts to make an impression. Instead, he recognized that it relied on something much more powerful—emotions. The campaign focused on awakening strong emotions in people, and Trump went viral every time he

Neuroscientists have identified similarities between social media use and drug or alcohol addiction. Likes and retweets give us a boost of confidence!

was online. It was like passing an accident on the roadway. America could not look away.

The impact that shares, tweets, and likes have on our brains, our emotions, and ultimately our behaviors, is strong. Neuroscientists discovered that social media has a significant effect on our neural networks and can motivate certain behaviors. By using brain-imaging studies, neuroscientists have identified similarities between social media use and drug or alcohol addiction.

Social information activates the brain's reward system. The instant stimulation of a like, a follow, or a retweet activates the reward system in our brains and leads to excitement in the form of dopamine release. This is similar to the reaction people have to drugs, cigarettes, and even gambling. For this reason, people often want to repeat the cycle, which keeps them engaged with social media.

This makes people extremely vulnerable to weaponization techniques like fake news and Russian-controlled sites. People are wired to believe rather than disbelieve, says science writer and historian Michael Shermer in a TED talk. He says this is especially true when people feel vulnerable. Consequently, people who weaponize social media—like politicians and governments—play into these feelings of anger and fearfulness to exploit them. In the end, it doesn't matter whether or not what they share is true as long as they can generate the right emotions. They will accomplish what they set out to do simply because our brains are hardwired to respond to their messages.[2]

What You Need to Remember About Weaponized Social Media

When something is weaponized, it is designed to create harm. It may be used to assassinate someone's character, create confusion, or spread misinformation. It also can be used to cause emotional or extreme responses from people.

Weaponizing social media should not be confused with satire or the sharing of political opinions. These are legitimate tools protected by the First Amendment. Experts point out that weaponized social media can impact free speech and other behaviors. In politics, this may mean critics no longer speak out. It also might undermine political campaigns and suppress votes.[3]

Tools of Weaponization

How are governments, businesses, and individuals weaponizing social media to sway opinions, push agendas, and exacerbate tensions in the country? Russian-controlled sites like "Heart of Texas" are just one example. Other ways social media is being weaponized include implementing bots, harvesting user data, creating deceptive advertising, and generating fake news.

Bots

Bots are computer programs that act like real people online and they are everywhere. But not all bots are bad. Bots help you

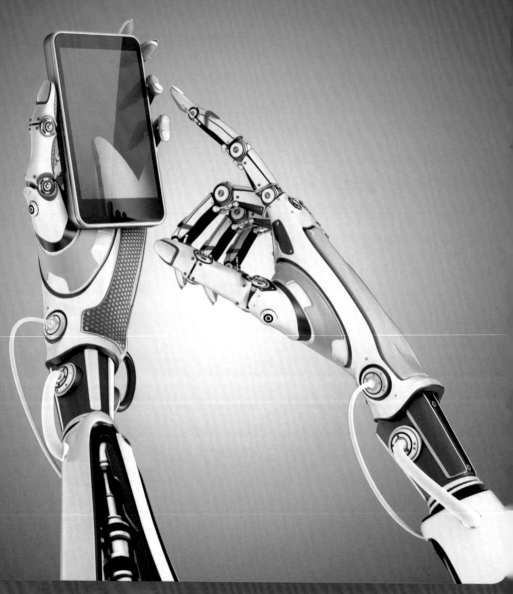

Not all bots are bad, but bots can be fake accounts run by algorithms designed to get you to click, be it a quiz, an advertisement, or a site that puts malware on your

with customer service online, and they help dictate messages on your smartphone. Each bot can be programmed with its own unique identity and purpose. There are bots designed for ad fraud, and there are bots designed to spread misinformation or propaganda.

"There are absolutely clever bots out there," explains Dan Kaminsky, a security researcher and the chief scientist of White Ops, a firm specializing in detecting malware activity. "But it's not like these are...wild, artificial intelligences. They're no more artificially intelligent than the printing press."

One example of how bots have been weaponized includes a Russian scam in which "bot farms" created thousands of fake websites. They used these websites to trick web marketers into buying millions of dollars' worth of video ads. Companies were willing to purchase the ads because they thought thousands of real people had viewed the ads. In reality, they were only bots designed to imitate real users on the web.

"They can [use bots to] create accounts that look like you and talk like you, which makes you more likely to believe [what is being posted]," says Clint Watts, a senior fellow at the Center for Cyber and Homeland Security at George Washington University. What's more, bots can be programmed to direct tweets at users with lots of followers and influence. By doing this, they are able to make false claims spread faster.[4]

User Data

From birthdays and hometowns, to where you spend your vacations, what you drive, and where you go to school, it's all out there for the world to see—and use. Every time you like a page, follow an organization, or share your favorite tune, algorithms chart your every move. Did you ever wonder how things you are most interested in always seem to pop up in your newsfeed? That's because social media's highly-sophisticated algorithms can predict what you might like based on how you spend your time online.

Initially, this sounds like a good thing. After all, you don't have to spend as much time searching for things. The problem is that hackers have figured out how to steal this data and use it to their advantage. They can develop ads, articles, and more that sway you in the direction they want you to go.

Fake News

Reputable news organizations are run by editors dedicated to reporting the truth, who want to build a solid reputation and avoid lawsuits. But when social media arrived, the rules changed.

Now, some journalists only look to create click-worthy headlines and monitor the success of their stories. It's even better if they are shared or liked.

Social media allows just about anyone to create and share fake news, says Toomas Hendrik Ilves, a fellow at Stanford University's Hoover Institution. He says that one study suggests that fake news shared before the November 2016 election had more views than real stories written by major news outlets.[5]

Impersonation/Fake Accounts

There are two ways that hackers impersonate people or companies online. The first is individual impersonation, or profile cloning. With this type of impersonation, the hacker uses fake accounts to pretend to be someone online. They might make malicious posts in the person's name, or they might spy on the user's social media accounts. Operatives from Russia used the tactic to monitor French president Emmanuel Macron's social media activity.

The other way hackers use impersonation as a tool is to create fake accounts that impersonate companies or brands, especially their customer support departments. People often try to impersonate Apple online, or they might try to impersonate a bank to get sensitive account information.

Spying

Users share a great deal of information about their lives with "friends" online. As a result, someone who is a friend or friend of a friend might be able to gather the following information: work and sleep schedule; friends, contacts, and family members; interests and hobbies; work history; and birthdate and possibly birthplace. The result is a rich profile for hackers to use when developing malicious posts, fake posts, and other types of clickbait.

Phishing/Malware

When hackers use phishing or malware on social media networks, they are trying to point you to an external link. You click on the link and leave the social media page and go to another site. Typically, the site is impersonating a company, brand, or organization in order to obtain your private information. The site also might install malware or viruses on your computer.

Once your account has been hijacked by the malware, it usually spreads to your contact list, where it attempts to hijack their information as well. It does this by sending a message, post, or email that looks like it is from you. Your friends and family are more likely to click on it because they trust you.[6]

Why Hackers Love Social Media

Many hackers see social media as an avenue for one-stop shopping when it comes to personal information. Compared to email, another popular channel of attack, social media gives hackers access to a great deal of information without ever having to take control or hack the account.

Most social networks are not overwhelmed with spam and marketing messages, like email can be. Users are often more comfortable on social networks and more willing to click on stories and ads. Most of the material they see is sent by friends, brands they trust, and organizations they have decided to follow. This creates a sense trust and community online.

In an experiment designed by researchers at ZeroFox, a social media security firm, a system automatically created and sent spear phishing links to Twitter users. What they found is that two-thirds of people clicked the bait.

"On tests consisting of 90 users, we found that our automated spear phishing framework had between a 30 percent and a 66 percent success rate," the team's report stated.

Hackers are different from trolls and bullies. They're usually after information, whether it be financial or otherwise.

Most people do not take the time to protect their personal information. Or worse, they share it freely. Depending on a person's privacy settings, hackers might be able to see everything from their contact list and location to their interest in music, books, and more. Compared to email, a hacker cannot see anything unless he breaches a person's account.

Anyone who wants to weaponize social media can gather information, tailor a campaign, and launch the campaign within the same social media site. With social media growing in popularity, the potential for attacks is growing. Until recently, email was the favorite mode of weaponization because nearly 90 percent of people in the US have an email account. But as social media continues to grow in popularity, it will be the new go-to tool for weaponization.[7]

Staying Safe: What You Need to Know About Weaponized Social Media

"*W*hich *superhero are you most like?*" "*What words do you use most often?*" "*Which Disney princess do you most resemble?*" These online quizzes can be fun to take and share, but that's also what makes them the ideal tools for scammers and hackers.

Quizzes posted to Facebook are especially worrisome because developers can use them to access personal details listed in your profile, or worse, lead you to fake websites that are part of a phishing scam. The safest option is to avoid them. But there are other ways to protect yourself, if you really can't help yourself. Make sure your privacy settings are as tight as possible, and do not list anything that isn't absolutely necessary in your profile.

If you do decide to take online quizzes and IQ tests, you need to realize that many of these are clickbait scams. What's more, many of them contain viruses that can damage your

"Which superhero are you?" "Which Disney princess is your soulmate?" Online quizzes are fun but are also a way for people to gather information about you.

computer, or phishing applications that attempt to steal your personal information.

"Almost everyone wants to test their skills in a short quiz, but...be skeptical if a post promises you something free that normally would cost money, such as an IQ test, a free credit score or 'exclusive' pictures of celebrities," says Michelle L. Correy, Better Business Bureau president and CEO. "The BBB advises consumers to be careful where they click."

The BBB offers the following tips to protect you from social media scams:

- Do not take the bait. Avoid ads, promotions, and stories that use the words "exclusive," "shocking," or "sensational."
- Hover over a link to see where the link will take you before you click. Do not click on links leading to unfamiliar websites.

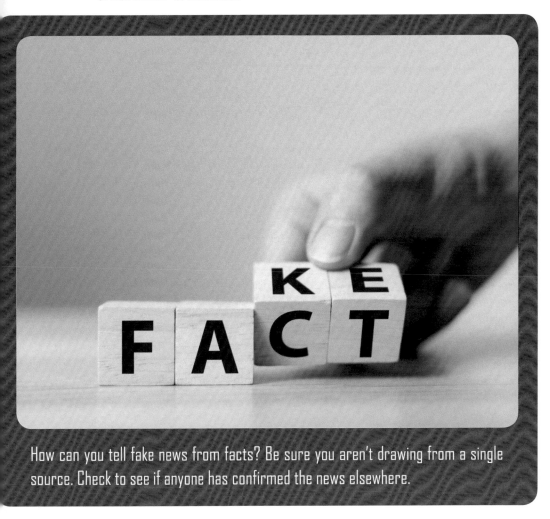

How can you tell fake news from facts? Be sure you aren't drawing from a single source. Check to see if anyone has confirmed the news elsewhere.

- Confirm that posts and articles are from your friends before clicking on them. Their account could have been hacked by scammers using a tactic called "clickjacking."
- Report scam posts, malware, or spam to appropriate social media sites.[1]

How to Spot Fake News Online

When it comes to news on social media, it is getting harder and harder to tell what is factual news and what is fake. Fake news stories are made to look real, and with their sensational headlines, and are often tempting to share and post. To make matters worse, a lot of people get their news from social media. According to the Pew Research Center, people under the age of fifty get half of their news online; and for those who are younger than thirty, online news is twice as popular as television news.

The chances of spreading misinformation are increasing, and it is important that you are able to distinguish between a factual and well-researched news story and one that is only made to look legitimate. Here are some tips for spotting fake news in your online news feed.

- **Check the domain name.** Look to see where the website is taking you before you click. For instance, some fake news stories will end in ".com.co"— abcnews.com is a real news site, but abcnews.com. co is not.
- **Google the author.** Try to find out if the person truly exits.

- **Pay attention to spelling errors.** Most writers and editors are diligent about proofreading and do not have many typos or mistakes in their work.
- **Where did the site come from?** Did the news show up as a direct message online? Is the news piece a story that is being promoted online? A lot of times, fake news will be nothing more than a flashy headline to get you to click.

Stay Safe and Secure

Explore ways to increase your account security and learn how we help protect you.

It's vital to stay safe online. Make sure your passwords are hard to guess and updated regularly, and make sure you're connected to people you trust.

Words to Live by—5 Tips for Safe Social Media Use

1. **Be authentic.** Do not pretend to be someone else online and do not go with the crowd, especially if they are shaming or cyberbullying someone.
2. **Be wary of strangers online.** Not everyone is who they say they are. It is easy for a fifty-year-old man to pose as a fourteen-year-old girl.
3. **Be careful when people ask to meet in person.** You should never agree to meet an online friend alone. Talk to your parents or other trusted adult first.
4. **Social media only shows what people want to show.** It is easy to see another person's posts and assume their life is exciting. But people only post what they want you to see.
5. **Be respectful online.** Treat other people the way you want to be treated.

- **Use a fact-checking site to check credibility.** Some good options include FactCheck.org and Snopes .com. Both sites do a good job of telling what is fact and what is fiction.[2]

Other Steps That Keep You Safe

When it comes to online safety, it's a matter of taking the proper steps for protection.

Passwords. Most social media accounts, email accounts, and others require a password. Be sure the passwords you select are hard for someone else to figure out, but are simple for you to remember.

Posting. When it comes to posting photos, videos, and other things online, it is important to remember your audience. You should not post or comment on anything with comments that might be used against you at some point.

People. Make sure you are connected to people who practice digital etiquette. If you are friends with people who cyberbully others or make rude or obnoxious posts, then others may associate you with them. When an online friend continues to overstep boundaries online, it may be a good idea to unfriend that person.

Photos. As soon as you post an image, you lose control over it. People can download it, share it, copy it, and even alter it. Photos often have geo-tags in them that identify exactly where you are or where you have been.

Privacy. Make sure your privacy settings are constantly up-to-date. Make sure that you are not sharing private or personal information that could be used to impersonate you.

When it comes to staying safe online and watching out for weaponized social media, you need to take some time and think about what you are doing. Does the site look reputable? Am I posting something that could hurt me or someone else? Is this quiz worth taking? Asking these questions will go a long way in helping prevent issues online.

Tools of the Trade: How Social Media Can Become a Positive Weapon

When Thea Linscott was diagnosed with cancer between her sophomore and junior years of high school, she never felt more alone. Although she had an amazing support group of friends and family surrounding her, no one really understood what she was going through. Years later, after Linscott had survived cancer, she stumbled across an online support network called "Stupid Cancer." It was an online support group she wishes she had as a teenager.

"This really is the organization I wish I had when I was diagnosed," says Linscott, who is now on the board of directors for Stupid Cancer. Stupid Cancer, which MTV calls "the dominant youth cancer nonprofit in the country," was founded to keep patients from feeling neglected and ignored.

Aside from exchanging information and stories, which can be empowering, the online group also teaches patients coping strategies. What's more, the anonymity and openness of social media is perfect for people who want to vent. As an added bonus, there is preliminary evidence that this online connection is creating positive outcomes for many patients.

Brad Love, a professor at the University of Texas in Austin who studies the psych-social outcomes of young adults with cancer, says that social media efforts like Stupid Cancer are an opportunity for improvement.

As frightening as the social media scene can be, it also provides an extraordinary way to connect with other people you might have never met otherwise.

Social media can also strengthen your local friendships because sometimes friends feel more comfortable typing something than saying something.

"We can fight social isolation," Love adds, saying that there is even data showing improved outcomes. "We are definitely seeing positive outcomes to the point that [the evidence] is above purely anecdotal." The next step he says is to develop studies that identify which forms of social media are helping people the most.[1]

Social Media Is Not All Bad

While there is much out there that points to the sinister use of social media and all the dangers that exist online, it is also important to realize that social media is not an inherently bad thing. In fact, there is a lot of good that comes from using social media. It only becomes a bad thing when people abuse it or weaponize it. In fact, research shows that there are numerous benefits to social media use. Here are the top ways you might benefit from using social media:

Social media can strengthen friendships.

Not only do friendships create a sense of belonging, but they also provide a level of support. Friendships help people feel empowered and connected to the world around them. When it comes to friendships and social media, it should come as no surprise that more than half of teens believe that it helps their friendships. According to a study conducted by Common Sense Media, 52 percent of teens felt that social media improved their friendships. Only 4 percent felt that social media harmed their friendships. The study also found that nearly 30 percent of social media users feel social media helps them feel more confident and outgoing.[2]

Emma Gonzalez, second from right, leads her fellow students in the #MarchForOurLives protests in the wake of the Parkland, Florida, school shooting.

Social media makes helping others or taking a stand easier.

Whether you are supporting an important cause, fundraising for a cancer patient, or raising money for a mission's trip, social media is a great tool for making an impact in your community. Take the #MarchForOurLives movement started by students in Parkland, Florida, as an example. During this march, students across the entire nation were able to come together in their effort to eliminate school shootings. With YouTube videos and Twitter campaigns, young adults are likely to continue to have an impact for years to come.

Social media can help teenagers feel like they belong.

While there are studies that indicate using social media can make people feel lonely, especially adults, there also is research indicating the opposite might be true for teenagers. In a study conducted by Griffith University and the University of Queensland in Australia, researchers discovered that even though teens report having fewer friends than teens did a decade ago, they report feeling less lonely. Experts suggest this might have to do with the impact of social media and technology.

One of the study's authors says that teens are able to find their niche online, which increases their self-esteem and sense of belonging. The study also found that teens are developing stronger social skills that might be related to social media use. As technology expands, strong online communications skills are becoming more important. In the end, this experience could make young adults strong communicators in the digital world.[3]

What Does Your Digital Footprint Say About You?

Making digital footprints is easy to do. With every photo on Instagram, every post to Facebook, and every tweet with your favorite hashtag, you leave a digital footprint unique to you. These footprints leave a trail that traces right back to you. Teachers, coaches, future employers, and college admissions officers can find them, and so can the people who are weaponizing social media. Are you leaving the kind of footprints that will help you build a platform and get noticed in positive ways? Or, are you leaving footprints that leak private information or could be used against you in some way?

Being able to manage, post, and interact with appropriate content online is an important life skill. You need to be able to distinguish between quality content and questionable content. Doing so will not only keep you safe online, but it also will help you stay informed.[6]

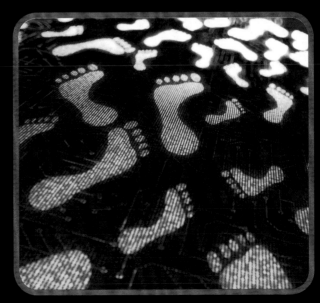

Every website you visit puts a small tracker called a cookie on your computer, creating a map of where you've been.

Social media lends support.

Years ago, teenagers like Linscott had trouble finding support for what they were going through. Likewise, teens struggling with their identity often felt marginalized and alone. This was especially true if there were no others like them in their schools or communities. With the birth of social media, teens are now able to connect with others like them all over the world. In return, they feel validated and more secure.

Teens can also find support for issues like eating disorders and drug addictions. Even teens contemplating suicide can find the support they need online to make a healthier choice. These areas of support are especially helpful for teens in remote areas where in-person support and resources might be limited.[4]

Social media helps build an online presence.

Using social media to build an online platform is an important skill if you want to get attention from college coaches, college admissions officers, and future employers. You can write blogs, develop YouTube videos, and create informational websites about things you love. You can also follow adults who work in industries you are interested in and retweet or repost their studies and articles. When done correctly, an online platform can help you build a positive online reputation that becomes a selling point on college and job applications.[5]

Social media provides a method of expression.

Whether you are interested in singing, writing, or building robots, social media provides an avenue for sharing your passions online. A teen who enjoys makeup trends and fashion can develop DIY videos, while another who enjoys crafting can develop a site on Etsy to sell their creations. Even those who enjoy video games are finding ways of sharing their passion for gaming online.

Research shows there is a direct relationship between self-expression and self-esteem. It gives you a way to be true to who you really are, which allows you to be content and comfortable in your own skin. When teens aren't able to express themselves and don't know anyone with the same interests, they start to question who they are and struggle with feeling different.

Social media helps you stay informed.

Many teens get their news and information online. From favorite celebrities and authors, to favorite brands and nonprofit groups, you can find everything you need with the click of a button. Forty percent of teens get their news from social media sites, according to a study by Common Sense Media, which interviewed nearly six hundred teens thirteen to eighteen years old.

Using social media as a news source has both pros and cons. While it is true that social media offers the speed and accessibility most are looking for, the downside is that anyone can post "news" stories online. You should be aware of the fact that not everything you read online is factual and take steps to verify what you read before accepting it as fact.

Social media does not have to be frightening. Even though it can be exploited by cyberbullies, trolls, and hackers hoping to weaponize it, if you keep online safety at the forefront of your interactions online, you can turn your social media experience into a positive one. Make sure you utilize the positive aspects of social media while remembering the dangers. By doing so, you will develop strong social media skills that will benefit you for years to come.

CHAPTER NOTES

Introduction

1. Booke Jarvis, "How One Woman's Digital Life Was Weaponized Against Her," *Wired*, November 14, 2017, https://www.wired.com/story/how-one-womans-digital-life-was-weaponized-against-her/ (accessed April 2018).
2. Amanda Lenhart, "Nonconsensual Image Sharing, Data & Society," December 13, 2016, https://datasociety.net/pubs/oh/Nonconsensual_Image_Sharing_2016.pdf (accessed April 2018).
3. Jarvis.

Chapter 1

Then and Now: A Closer Look at Social Media

1. "The History of Social Media: Social Networking Revolution," History Cooperative, http://historycooperative.org/the-history-of-social-media/ (accessed April 2018).
2. "American Teens Are Taking Breaks from Social Media; Some Step Back Deliberately, but Other Breaks Are Involuntary," Associated Press-NORC Center for Public Affairs Research, http://www.apnorc.org/projects/Pages/

HTML%20Reports/american-teens-are-taking-breaks-from-social-media.aspx (accessed April 2018).

3. Carrie Kerpen, "How Has Social Media Changed Us?," *Forbes*, April 21, 2016, https://www.forbes.com/sites/carriekerpen/2016/04/21/how-has-social-media-changed-us/#4b117edb5dfc (accessed April 2018).

4. Wayne Lonstein, "Weaponizing Social Media: New Technology Brings New Threats," *Forbes*, July 24, 2017, https://www.forbes.com/sites/forbestechcouncil/2017/07/24/weaponizing-social-media-new-technology-brings-new-threats/#4a50799434fa (accessed April 2018).

5. Booke Jarvis, "How One Woman's Digital Life Was Weaponized Against Her," *Wired*, November 14, 2017, https://www.wired.com/story/how-one-womans-digital-life-was-weaponized-against-her/ (accessed April 2018).

Chapter 2

Getting Off Track: The Impact of Weaponized Social Media

1. "Technology Is Like a Bomb: Social Media Weaponized in Myanmar's Rohingya Crisis," February 23, 2018, https://www.cbsnews.com/news/rohingya-refugee-crisis-myanmar-weaponizing-social-media-preview/ (accessed April 2018).

2. Eric Westevelt, "How Russia Weaponized Social Media with 'Social Bots,'" NPR, November 5, 2017, https://www.npr.org/2017/11/05/562058208/how-russia-weaponized-social-media-with-social-bots (accessed April 2018).

3. Matthew Rosenberg, "How Trump Consultants Exploited the Facebook Data of Millions," *New York Times*, March 17, 2018, https://www.nytimes.com/2018/03/17/us/politics/cambridge-analytica-trump-campaign.html (accessed April 2018).

4. David Golumbia, "Social Media Has Hijacked Our Brains and Threatens Global Democracy," Motherboard, January 5, 2018, https://motherboard.vice.com/en_us/article/bjy7ez/social-media-threatens-global-democracy (accessed April 2018).

5. Hillary Grigonis, "Social (Net)Work: How Does Social Media Influence Democracy," Digital Trends, March 21, 2018, https://www.digitaltrends.com/social-media/how-does-social-media-influence-democracy/ (accessed April 2018).

6. Golumbia.

Chapter 3

Online Danger Zone: How Social Media Is Weaponized by Teens

1. Francie Diep, "Confronting My Cyberbully, 13 Years Later," *The Atlantic*, September 20, 2014, https://www.theatlantic.com/technology/archive/2014/09/confronting-my-cyberbully-thirteen-years-later/380888/ (accessed April 2018).

2. Sherri Gordon, "Signs Social Media Is Ruining Teen Friendships," Verywell Family, February 12, 2018, https://

www.verywellfamily.com/signs-social-media-is-ruining-teen-friendships-460643 (accessed April 2018).

3. Sherri Gordon, "6 Types of Cyberbullying," Verywell Family, February 13, 2018, https://www.verywellfamily.com/types-of-cyberbullying-460549 (accessed April 2018).

4. Sherri Gordon, "How to Deal with Internet Trolls," Verywell Family, April 13, 2018, https://www.verywellfamily.com/how-to-deal-with-internet-trolls-4161018 (accessed April 2018).

Chapter 4

Information Warfare: How Social Media Is Being Weaponized by Governments, Politicians, and Businesses

1. Casey Michel, "How the Russians Pretended to Be Texans and Texans Believed Them," *Washington Post*, October 17, 2017, https://www.washingtonpost.com/news/democracy-post/wp/2017/10/17/how-the-russians-pretended-to-be-texans-and-texans-believed-them/?utm_term=.4eaac57b8f24 (accessed April 2018).

2. Lauren Migliore, "(Anti-)Social Media: How Social Networks Affect Our Neural Networks," *Brain World Magazine*, February 28, 2018, http://brainworldmagazine.com/anti-social-media-social-networks-affect-neural-networks/ (accessed April 2018).

3. Alan Rosenblatt, Ph.D., "Weaponizing Social Media," *Huffington Post*, April 10, 2017, https://www.

huffingtonpost.com/entry/weaponizing-social-media_
us_58ebad34e4b0145a227cb6f1 (accessed April 2018).

4. Eric Westervelt, "How Russia Weaponized Social Media with Social Bots," NPR, November 5, 2017, https://www.npr. org/2017/11/05/562058208/how-russia-weaponized-social-media-with-social-bots (accessed April 2018).

5. Hillary Grigonis, "Social (Net)Work: How Does Social Media Influence Democracy," Digital Trends, March 21, 2018, https://www.digitaltrends.com/social-media/how-does-social-media-influence-democracy/ (accessed April 2018).

6. "Social Media Threats: Facebook, Malware, Twitter, Phishing and More," Calyptix Security, https://www.calyptix.com/ top-threats/social-media-threats-facebook-malware-twitter-phishing/ (accessed April 2018).

7. Ibid.

Chapter 5

Staying Safe: What You Need to Know About Weaponized Social Media

1. Better Business Bureau, "BBB Warns Consumers of Facebook IQ Test Traps," Better Business Bureau, January 21, 2016, https://www.bbb.org/stlouis/news-events/news-releases/2016/01/bbb-advises-caution-with-facebook-iq-tests/ (accessed April 2018).

2. Christina Nagler, "4 Tips for Spotting a Fake News Story," Harvard Summer School, Harvard University, 2017, https://

www.summer.harvard.edu/inside-summer/4-tips-spotting-fake-news-story (accessed April 2018).

Chapter 6

Tools of the Trade: How Social Media Can Become a Positive Weapon

1. Kristine Crane, "How Social Media Helps Young People with Cancer," *U.S. News & World Report*, December 4, 2014, https://health.usnews.com/health-news/patient-advice/articles/2014/12/04/how-social-media-helps-young-people-with-cancer (accessed April 2018).

2. "Social Media, Social Life: How Teens View Their Digital Lives," Common Sense Media, June 26, 2012, https://www.commonsensemedia.org/research/social-media-social-life-how-teens-view-their-digital-lives (accessed April 2018).

3. "Declining Loneliness Among American Teenagers," Society for Personality and Social Psychology, November 24, 2014, http://www.spsp.org/news-center/press-releases/declining-loneliness-among-american-teenagers (accessed April 2018).

4. Sherri Gordon, "Surprising Ways Your Teen Benefits from Social Media," Verywell Family, February 8, 2018, https://www.verywellfamily.com/benefits-of-social-media-4067431 (accessed April 2018).

5. Ibid.

6. Sherri Gordon, "4 Reasons Digital Literacy Skills Are Important for Kids," Verywell Family, February 9, 2018,

https://www.verywellfamily.com/why-digital-literacy-skills-are-important-4106612 (accessed April 2018).

7. "What Are Teens Primary News Sources," Marketing Charts, March 16, 2017, https://www.marketingcharts.com/industries/media-and-entertainment-75562 (accessed April 2018).

GLOSSARY

algorithm A set of rules or calculations that a computer follows in order to gather data.

anonymizer A tool designed to make activity on the internet untraceable.

blog A personal web log where people share about their life, their work.

bot A computer program that acts like a real person online.

catfishing When someone develops a fake persona online and attempts to lure another person into a fake relationship.

clickbait Online content with the sole purpose of enticing people to click on the material provided.

clickjacking A technique hackers and scammers use where hyperlinks are hidden behind legitimate copy online.

dopamine A chemical in the body that communicates with the brain's reward system signaling when something is pleasurable.

hacker A person who uses computers and other technology to gain access to private data and information online.

malware Software that is designed to infect and often disable a computer.

phishing Websites and emails that look legitimate but are designed to steal personal information.

propaganda Information that is often false or misleading that is designed to spread a political goal or a particular point of view.

protection order An order issued by police designed to protect people and businesses from a person who has harmed them or threatened to harm them.

satire The use of humor or exaggeration to draw attention to issues in politics or with certain points of view.

troll A person who disrupts conversations online and creates chaos by posting false, accusing, or inflammatory material.

FURTHER READING

Books

Fromm, Megan. *Privacy and Digital Security*. New York, NY: Rosen Young Adult, 2015.

Hand, Carol. *Everything You Need to Know About Fake News and Propaganda*. New York, NY: Rosen Young Adult, 2018.

McKee, Jonathan. *The Teen's Guide to Social Media and Mobile Devices: 21 Tips to Wise Posting in an Insecure World*. Uhrichsville, OH: Shiloh Run Press, 2017.

Yearling, Trisha. *How Do I Keep My Privacy Online?* New York, NY: Enslow Publishing, 2016.

Websites

Common Sense Media
www.commonsensemedia.org
Common Sense is a nonprofit organization dedicated to helping kids navigate social media and technology.

FactCheck.org
www.factcheck.org
This nonpartisan, consumer advocate group monitors the factual accuracy of what is said by major US politicians.

MediaSmarts
mediasmarts.ca
MediaSmarts is a Canadian not-for-profit organization that promotes digital and media literacy.

INDEX